Festivals *of the* *World*

INDONESIA

Gareth Stevens Publishing
MILWAUKEE

Written by
ELIZABETH BERG

Designed by
HASNAH MOHD ESA

Picture research by
SUSAN JANE MANUEL

First published in North America in 1997 by
Gareth Stevens Publishing
1555 North RiverCenter Drive, Suite 201
Milwaukee, Wisconsin 53212 USA

For a free color catalog describing Gareth
Stevens' list of high-quality books and multimedia
programs, call
1-800-542-2595 (USA)
or 1-800-461-9120 (Canada).
Gareth Stevens Publishing's Fax: (414) 225-0377.
See our catalog, too, on the World Wide Web:
http://gsinc.com

© TIMES EDITIONS PTE LTD 1997
Originated and designed by
Times Books International
an imprint of Times Editions Pte Ltd
Times Centre, 1 New Industrial Road
Singapore 536196
Printed in Singapore

Library of Congress Cataloging-in-Publication Data:
Berg, Elizabeth, 1953–
Indonesia / by Elizabeth Berg.
p. cm. — (Festivals of the world)
Includes bibliographical references and index.
Summary: Describes how the culture of Indonesia
is reflected in its festivals, including Sekatan,
Good Friday, and Fahombe.
ISBN 0-8368-1933-0 (library binding)
1. Indonesia—Civilization—Juvenile literature.
2 Festivals—Indonesia—Juvenile literature.
[1. Festivals—Indonesia. 2. Indonesia—Social life
and customs.] I. Title. II. Series.
DS625.B39 1997
959.8—dc21   97-2865

1 2 3 4 5 6 7 8 9 01 00 99 98 97

CONTENTS

4 **Where's Indonesia?**

6 **When's the Selamatan?**

8 **Sekaten**

12 **Odalan**

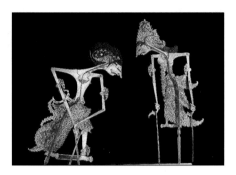

16 **Sending off the Dead**

20 **Good Friday and Caci**

24 **Fahombe**

26 **Things For You To Do**
★ **Make a Shadow Puppet**
★ **Make Fried Tempeh**

32 **Glossary and Index**

It's Festival Time . . .

Indonesians love a festival. In Java they call a festival a *selamatan* [sell-AH-mah-tahn]—a feast where the whole village eats together. They do this whenever they get the chance because it brings good luck. And what's a feast without a shadow puppet play and gamelan music to go with it? And while we're at it, how about some dances? And don't forget the procession. Come on, it's festival time in Indonesia . . .

WHERE'S INDONESIA?

Indonesia is the largest archipelago in the world. It is composed of five main islands—Sumatra, Java, Kalimantan, Sulawesi, and Irian Jaya—and 13,000 smaller islands. Its territory lies across the equator, so the weather is

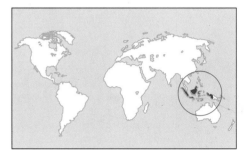

hot and humid all year long. Most of the islands were formed from volcanoes that rose up from the seabed, so the land is very mountainous. Many active volcanoes still exist in Indonesia.

Who are the Indonesians?

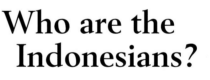

Indonesia has the fifth largest population of any country in the world, just after the United States. Most of those people live on Java. There are over 300 different peoples in Indonesia, and Indonesians speak over 250 languages. What a lot of different peoples and cultures! The people follow four of the world's major religions—Islam, Hinduism, Buddhism, and Christianity—but most Indonesians are Muslim.

A friendly Javanese girl.

INDESIA

N

South China Sea

MALAYSIA

SINGAPORE

Sulawesi Sea

MALUKU
ISLANDS

NIAS

SUMATRA

KALIMANTAN

SULAWESI

IRIAN JAYA

PAPUA NEW GUINEA

Indian
Ocean

Java Sea

Jakarta
Cirebon
Borobudur
Yogyakarta   Surabaya
JAVA

BALI

FLORES

Banda Sea

Arafura Sea

TIMOR

Java Trench

Borobudur is a
Buddhist temple on
Java that was built
about 1,200 years
ago when the
Javanese were
Buddhist.

WHEN'S THE SELAMATAN?

Because Indonesia includes so many different peoples and religions, there are many festivals to celebrate. There are also several calendars. Muslims follow a lunar calendar that is 11 days shorter than the Western calendar. Their festivals fall on different dates every year. The Balinese use a calendar that has 210 days in the year. Their festivals come around every 210 days. Some other festivals follow the Western calendar.

MUSLIM HOLIDAYS

✪ **SEKATEN**

✪ **LEBARAN**—Also known as Eid al-Fitr, this holiday marks the end of the fasting month of Ramadan.

✪ **EID AL-ADHA**—People celebrate Ibrahim's (Abraham to Christians) willingness to sacrifice his son. Animals are sacrificed on the grounds of the mosque, and the meat is handed out to the people.

BALINESE HOLIDAYS

- **NYEPI**—The Balinese New Year, when no fires are lit, no work done, and no one leaves the home. Everyone stays totally silent for the day in the hope that visiting demons will think Bali is deserted.
  On the eve of Nyepi, offerings are left for demons that live at crossroads. As darkness falls, everyone comes out into the streets with gongs, cymbals, and torches. They make as much noise as possible to chase away any demons.
- **GALUNGAN**—This celebrates the 10 days when gods and ancestors return to earth. Decorations and offerings are left outside temples and homes.
- **ODALAN**

Yummy! (On page 13).

SEASONAL HOLIDAYS

- **INDEPENDENCE DAY** (August 17)—Celebrates Indonesia's independence from the Netherlands. Boys and girls representing the different provinces receive flags from the president.
- **KARTINI DAY** (April 21)—Honors Raden Ajeng Kartini, one of Indonesia's most respected national heroes. She fought for women's right to be educated. On this day, women are honored, and men do the housework.
- **EASTER**
- **MADURA BULL RACES**—Bulls are fed a special diet of beer, eggs, and chili peppers to prepare them for the big September races.

For a really wild ride, come to the Madura Bull Races!

SEKATEN

I n Java, the biggest festival of the year celebrates Prophet
Muhammad's birthday. The Javanese call it Sekaten [seh-KAH-
ten]. In Yogyakarta, a *gamelan* [GAH-meh-lahn] (a traditional
Indonesian orchestra) that stays in the *kraton* [KRA-tawn] is brought
to the Great Mosque. A special gamelan concert is put on in the
mosque before thousands of people. A few days later, a procession of
palace guards and other important people escorts the gamelan back to
the kraton. Afterward, specially prepared rice is handed out to the
crowd. This rice is supposed to bring good fortune.

This is a Javanese gamelan. In many
villages, the whole town turns out to
play in gamelan practices, or at least
to listen.

What is a gamelan?

A gamelan is made up of between five and
40 instruments, mostly different kinds of
percussion instruments. The instruments
with the lowest sound (like the gongs) keep
the basic beat, while the xylophones carry the
melody. The other instruments (like bamboo
flutes, zithers, and small gongs) add extra
sound. Each musician plays one rhythm over
and over. When they are all put together, the
music is wonderful to listen to.

Opposite: A Sekaten procession
includes many beautiful offerings.

The *serimpi* [seh-RIM-pee] is a court dance that was once performed only by princesses. In the dance, two Amazons move together, fighting with little daggers or other weapons.

Royal dances

You might also see some dance performances at Sekaten. Javanese dance is slow, stately, and dignified. The royal courts all used to have palace dance and theater groups that performed for the **sultan** (the ruler) on special occasions. The *Bedoyo Ketawang* [beh-DOY-yoh keh-TAH-wang] is a special dance performed once a year. It is very sacred because the Javanese believe that the powerful Goddess of the South Sea comes to the performance and marries the sultan afterward. Until recently, no outsiders were allowed to see the dance. Dancers may practice only once every five weeks on a special day.

Opposite: This gamelan player is wearing traditional Javanese dress, with a *kris* [kuh-REES] tucked into the back of his *sarong* [SAH-rong]. A sarong is a piece of fabric that is wrapped around the waist.

10

A shadow puppet master at work. The puppet master does all the voices, while a gamelan provides the music. He makes up the dialogue as he goes along.

Want to see a shadow play?

A special part of Indonesian festivals is the *wayang kulit* [WAH-yahng KOO-lit], or shadow puppet play. The puppet master sits behind a screen with the puppets (there may be hundreds of them for a performance). A light behind him throws the shadows of the puppets onto the screen. People can sit in front of the screen and watch the shadows or behind it and watch the puppet master. The stories are traditional, but the puppet master usually adds to them. Shadow plays start at 9:00 at night and go on until dawn.

Think about this

Sekaten is a Muslim festival, but the way it is celebrated is more Indonesian than Muslim. Do you know how people celebrate Prophet Muhammad's birthday in other countries?

Sword play

Sekaten is the only day of the year when Indonesians can make a *kris*. What's a kris, you ask? A kris is a very special knife with a curved blade, which Indonesian men carry on ceremonial occasions. They believe it is magical. In fact, the kris is so important that it was once used to represent a man when he couldn't come in person to his wedding.

11

ODALAN

Bali is famous for its beautiful festivals. Every 210 days, a Balinese temple has a birthday, or odalan. For the temple's birthday, the village holds its biggest festival of the year. Everyone goes to the temple carrying trays piled high with food on their heads. The food is an offering to the gods. Statues of the gods kept in the temple are taken down to the sea in a colorful procession. After returning to the temple, the gods are presented with offerings. Finally, everyone sits down to a big feast.

A little girl plays the role of the daughter of a god in an odalan procession.

What are their beliefs?

The Balinese are Hindus. The Hindu religion was brought to Bali many centuries ago by Indian traders. Like Hindus in India, the Balinese worship many gods. But the Balinese have their own ways of doing things, and the way they practice their religion is very different from other Hindus.

Taking the temple statues to the sea to be cleansed. People pour water over them to purify them, and then everyone is blessed.

Building up the life force

During an odalan, many Indonesians hold feasts for the entire village to strengthen what they call **semangat** [seh-MAHN-gaht]. Semangat is the life force that runs through people, plants, animals, special objects, and even entire villages or countries. There is semangat in good beings as well as in evil beings. It is important to make sure your own semangat and that of your village are strong enough to overcome the evil creatures that inhabit the world.

What happens next?

In the evening the party begins. There are dance performances and shadow puppet plays, and sometimes plays with wooden puppets. The music and entertainment go on all night long. Children often fall asleep. Even adults may doze off from time to time, but they wake up for the exciting parts. When the sun comes up, everyone goes out to worship the sun. Then they all go home to sleep.

Women carry offerings to the temple. Could you carry a big tray of offerings like this on your head? Could you do it without using your hands?

Opposite: Maybe you'll see a *kecak* [KEH-chak] dance in Bali. The kecak, or Monkey Dance, was made up not too long ago. A group of 150 men sit in a circle and make rhythms that imitate gamelan music. Sometimes they sound like monkeys chattering. In the center, two actors put on a play.

A legong dancer shows off her delicate hand movements. Her headdress is decorated with frangipani blossoms, and she is covered from head to toe in gold cloth.

Want to dance?

Everyone likes to see a *legong* [leh-GONG] dance, so it's part of many Balinese festivals. Traditionally, only little girls dance the legong. Girls start learning to dance when they are very young in Bali. By the time they are 10 or so, they are very good dancers. When they get to be about 13 or 14, it's time to retire. The legong takes a lot of practice and training because each movement and gesture has its own meaning and must be done exactly right.

Watch out for Rangda!

The Balinese often perform a dance to show the struggle between good and evil. In this dance, a good beast called the barong fights with the evil witch, Rangda. A group of men armed with kris try to kill Rangda. She takes control of them and makes them turn their swords back on themselves. Finally, the barong saves them and kills Rangda.

The barong (at left) is all white, with a long white beard. Rangda is at the right. You can see her long fingernails, huge fangs, and long tongue.

Think about this

The Balinese also like gamelan music and shadow puppet plays, but they have their own style in both. While the Javanese performances are stately and dignified, the Balinese are loud, exciting, and colorful.

SENDING OFF THE DEAD

The Balinese believe that the soul lives forever, and the body is only a shell that holds it for awhile. When someone dies, their body is burned and their soul is released so they can be **reincarnated**. That means they return to another life in a different form. Death is not a sad event for the Balinese because the person who has died is going on to a new and better life. Funerals performed for the dead are joyful events—some of the most colorful occasions to take place in Bali.

A performer dressed to entertain the people at a **cremation** ceremony.

Opposite: The body is put in a large animal figure. Here it is a black bull. The men of the village carry the body to the cremation grounds. They run and turn in circles to confuse the soul so it won't be able to find its way back and bother the living.

A wild ride

The dead must be given a proper send-off to ensure that they get started properly in their next life. The body is lifted over the wall instead of taken through the front gate. That way, the soul won't be able to find its way back to the house. The body is then put on a big tower, which is carried by up to 100 men. Younger relatives of the dead often ride on the tower with the body. Music and amusement are also part of the procession. When they get to the cremation grounds, the relatives have a last look at the body. Then the tower is set on fire. When everything has burned, the ashes are collected in a coconut shell. The family takes the ashes down to the sea at sunset and sprinkles them over the water. Then everyone bathes and returns home, happy that their loved one is now free.

Above: The body goes up in flames, while *(opposite)* family members and friends enjoy a big feast. The food is spread out on banana leaves, which is what Indonesians usually use for plates.

Below: A cremation procession goes through the water on its way to a temple near the beach.

Think about this

For some people, a funeral is a sad occasion, but for many it is a time to celebrate life. In Ireland, the dead are sent off with a big party where people eat and drink all night long.

GOOD FRIDAY AND CACI

The island of Flores is, like most of Indonesia, a mixture of many different peoples and beliefs. Often the same people follow more than one religion. Most people on Flores are Catholic, but they also hold on to old traditions from a time before Catholicism came to the island. Even if a person considers himself to be Catholic, he may also sacrifice chickens to keep certain spirits happy. Let's visit the village of Larantuka for Good Friday (that's the day when Jesus Christ was crucified).

When the Good Friday procession stops at an altar, a girl holds up a painting of Christ and sings a beautiful song. She is playing the role of Veronica, who mourned Christ when she uncovered his grave.

Good Friday on Flores

Good Friday is a solemn occasion in Larantuka. At midnight, Catholics stage a barefoot procession through the streets of Flores. Lit by torches and candles, the procession is very dramatic. The marchers carry a statue of the Virgin Mary that washed up on the shores of the island long ago. They also carry a box draped in black that has a statue inside. It represents Jesus's coffin. The men carrying the coffin wear white robes with tall, pointed red hats. The sound of muffled drums keeps the rhythm for the marchers.

A procession escorts a box through the candlelit streets. The costumes look like those worn for Good Friday in Portugal. Flores was once a colony of Portugal.

Lighting candles to celebrate the resurrection of Christ.

21

Another side of Flores

While East Flores celebrates Good Friday, let's go over to West Flores and see a whip duel. A celebration on Flores wouldn't be complete without a whip duel, called a *caci* [CHA-chee]. In the duel, two men are given long leather whips and shields made of buffalo hide. They face each other, and each tries to slash the other with his whip. The whips flick quickly, leaving bloody marks on the bare backs of the fighters. In the end, the fighter who draws the most blood wins. The men of Flores proudly show off scars earned in whip duels. Their scars represent bravery.

Two whip fighters battle it out. They wear head coverings to protect their heads, but only their skill protects their backs.

Women provide the music for a whip duel. They add to the excitement by drumming faster and faster.

Offerings to spirits

By the end of a whip duel, the fighters' backs are covered with blood. Traditionally, people thought of this blood as an offering to the spirits of the dead, called *nitu* [NEE-too]. Many people on Flores still believe that nitu live in trees, rivers, mountains, and other natural things. This is called **animism**. Animists believe there are spirits in nature. They offer gifts to make sure the spirits help them.

Every man adopts a fighting name for whip duels. Do you think this man is Wild Boar or Rearing Horse or Naughty Rooster? Or maybe Gone Around The World And Yet To Be Beat?

Think about this

Many Indonesians continue to worship nature in some way even though they are Christian or Muslim or Hindu. Instead of giving up their old beliefs, they combine them with their new religion. Do you know of other people who do this?

FAHOMBE

On Nias Island, near the coast of Sumatra, the big celebration is saved for young men coming of age. They call this Fahombe [fah-HOHM-bay]. There are coming-of-age celebrations in many parts of Indonesia. These festivals have been around for a long time. On Nias, a young man must prove his worth by leaping over a stone column two feet (60 cm) wide and several yards (2–3 m) high.

This used to be a preparation for the warrior life, when he would have to jump over enemy walls with a torch in one hand and an axe in the other. Today, it is just for fun.

A Nias chief sits on his throne.

Opposite: A young man in mid-flight. Until recently, Nias Island has been very isolated. People there still follow the same way of life as they have for hundreds of years.

THINGS FOR YOU TO DO

Indonesians, in case you haven't noticed, love art of all kinds—music, dance, painting, theater, puppets, masks. What? You haven't heard about masks? Let's talk about masks. There's a special dance in many parts of Indonesia, but especially on Bali and Java. It's called Topeng, the Masked Dance. For Topeng, a dancer puts on a mask and acts as that character would. Simple. Now it's your turn.

Dance the Topeng

Imagine a character. It could be someone you know or someone you've made up. How would that character walk and talk? What would he or she wear? What about gestures? Now think about your character's face and make a mask that shows what it is like. Use a piece of cardboard and paint a face on it, or get creative and make a papier-mâché mask with hair. The masks on these pages may give you some ideas. Then put on a performance.

Topeng in Cirebon

Cirebon (that's a town on Java) is known for its colorful Topeng dance. It was once put on as part of weddings or when people planted or harvested rice. (Rice is very important on Java, which is mostly covered with rice fields.) Topeng dancers don't tell a story—they act out characters. Usually they're funny characters. The one with the red face on this page is Rahwana. She is always angry and stomps around the stage with an evil "ho, ho, ho." There are lots of others, too. A Topeng dancer might have 25 or 30 masks. The dancers use the masks to show how silly people can be.

Add some music, too

Oh yes, you'll also need a gamelan to go along with your dance—maybe your friends could bang on some drums for you? Have fun!

Things to look for in your library

Ayu and the Perfect Moon. David Cox (Random House, 1989).
Indonesia. (Ambrose Video Publishing).
The Indonesia Experience. (International Video Network).
Javanese Court Gamelan (Nonesuch Records, 1971).
Letters of a Javanese Princess. Raden Adjeng Kartini (University Press of America, 1985).
The Magic Crocodile and other Folktales from Indonesia. Charlene K. Smoyer and Alice M. Terada (University of Hawaii Press, 1995).
Music from the Morning of the World (Nonesuch Records, 1988).
Where is Indonesia? Pat Ryan (Child's World, 1997).

MAKE A SHADOW PUPPET

Make your own shadow puppet (or a few of them!), and put on a play. We have used a traditional character that appears in all shadow plays, but you can use your imagination and make your puppet look totally different.

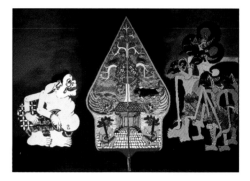

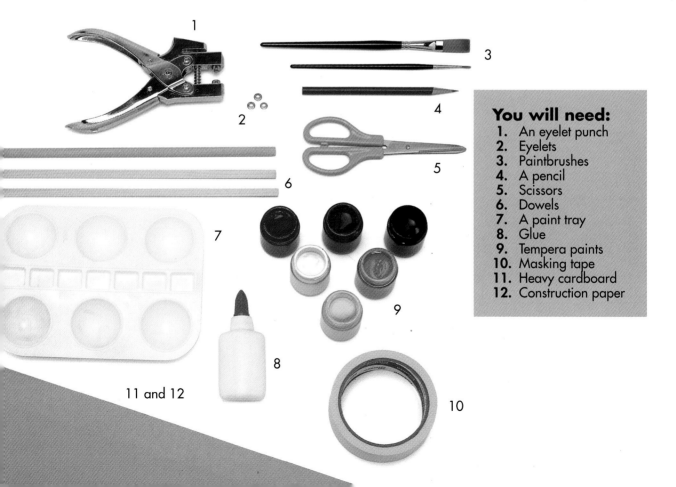

You will need:
1. An eyelet punch
2. Eyelets
3. Paintbrushes
4. A pencil
5. Scissors
6. Dowels
7. A paint tray
8. Glue
9. Tempera paints
10. Masking tape
11. Heavy cardboard
12. Construction paper

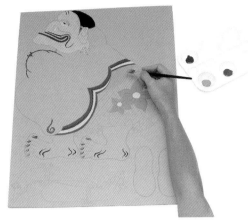

1 Draw the shadow puppet's body and arms onto the piece of cardboard and paint the body in bright colors. Draw the arms separately and in two pieces (the upper and lower arms) so they can bend.

2 Cut the pieces out.

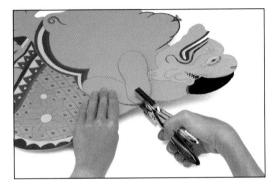

3 Make holes in the elbows and shoulders and use eyelets to attach the arms.

4 Tape the dowels to the back of the hands. You will use these to move the arms. Use a white sheet to make a screen. Put a light behind it and put on a shadow play!

MAKE FRIED TEMPEH

Tempeh is an Indonesian speciality. It is made of fermented soybeans that are pressed into a cake. After you fry it, it tastes like meat. Indonesians often use a banana leaf as a plate and eat with their fingers. Try it!

You will need:
1. 1 package tempeh
2. 1 clove garlic
3. ¹/₂ teaspoon ground coriander
4. 1 tablespoon soy sauce
5. 6 tablespoons butter
6. A frying pan
7. A cutting board
8. A knife
9. A fork
10. Measuring spoons

1 Slice the tempeh into ¹/₄-inch slices. (The tempeh we used here is the way it looks in Indonesia—yours may look a little different.)

2 Chop the garlic into very small bits (or use a garlic press).

3 Melt the butter in a frying pan. Add the garlic and coriander and fry until golden (about one minute).

4 Add the tempeh. Dribble soy sauce over the tempeh and fry until browned. Use the fork to turn them over and fry the other side. Serve with some rice.

GLOSSARY

animism, 23   The belief that there are spirits in nature.
cremation, 16   Burning the body of a dead person.
gamelan, 8   A group of percussion instruments originally from Java.
kraton, 8   Royal palace.
kris, 11   A short knife with a curved blade.
mosque, 8   A Muslim temple.
percussion, 8   Instruments struck to produce musical sounds.
reincarnated, 16   The souls of the dead returning in another form.
selamatan, 3   A feast for the whole village.
semangat, 13   Life force.
sultan, 10   Ruler.
wayang kulit, 11   Shadow puppet plays.

INDEX

animism, 23

Bali, 6, 7, 12–19
barong, 15
Bedoyo Ketawang, 10
Buddhism, 4, 5

Christianity, 4, 20–23
cremation, 16, 19

dances, 3, 10, 13, 14–15, 26–27

Fahombe, 24–25
Flores, 20–23

gamelan, 3, 8, 11, 14, 15, 27
Good Friday, 20–21

Hinduism, 4, 12

Islam, 4, 6, 8, 11

Java, 4, 5, 8, 10

Kartini Day, 7
kecak, 14–15
kris, 10, 11, 15

Lebaran, 6
legong, 14

Madura Bull Races, 7

Nias Island, 24–25
Nyepi, 7

odalan, 7, 12–15

Sekaten, 6, 8–11

serimpi, 10
shadow puppets, 3, 11, 13, 15, 28–29
Sumatra, 4, 24

Topeng, 26–27

whip duel, 22–23

Picture Credits
Photobank Singapore: 3 (top), 6, 7 (both), 8, 10, 11 (top), 12 (both), 14, 15 (both), 20, 21 (both), 22, 23 (both), 24, 28; Image Bank: 2, 3 (bottom), 5, 19 (top), 26, 27; Jill Gocher: 9, 11, 13; BES Stock: 16, 17; Hutchison Library: 19 (bottom), 25; HBL: 1; Harry Pariser: 4; Victor Englebert: 18.